Pamper Me to Hell & Back
Hera Lindsay Bird

smith|doorstop

Published 1st February 2018 by
Smith|Doorstop Books
The Poetry Business
Campo House
54 Campo Lane
Sheffield S1 2EG

Copyright © Hera Lindsay Bird 2018
All Rights Reserved

ISBN 978-1-910367-84-1

Designed and Typeset by Camilla Lovell Design
Printed by Biddles Books

Smith|Doorstop Books are a member of Inpress: www.inpressbooks.co.uk.
Distributed by NBN International, Airport Business Centre, 10 Thornbury
Road, Plymouth, PL6 7PP

The Poetry Business gratefully acknowledges the support
of Arts Council England.

Contents

5	Bruce Willis you are the ghost
6	Speech time
9	I will already remember you for the rest of my life
10	Everything is about to go wrong forever
12	I want to get high my whole life with you
14	Waste my life
16	Jealousy
17	I am so in love with you I want to lie down in the middle of a major public intersection and cry
19	I knew I loved you when you showed me your Minecraft World
20	Watching six seasons of the Nanny while my long-term relationship slowly fell apart
22	I have come back from the dead to tell you that I love you
23	Untitled 404
25	Pyramid scheme

For RWT

Bruce Willis you are the ghost

It's not that your wife doesn't love you. It's because you died and now you're a ghost and she can't hear you talking to her. That time you saw her taking off her wedding ring? It's because you're her dead husband and she can't continue to mourn your absence with heterosexual jewellery indefinitely. Stop haunting her already Bruce Willis! Bruce Willis, it's hard to be a ghost and not know you are a ghost. Haven't you noticed the only person you've talked to in a year is a supernaturally gifted child? Don't you think it's weird your wife just cries alone in the living room every night, re-watching your wedding tape and never looking or speaking to you? Don't you remember being fatally shot in the stomach at the beginning of the movie? Walk towards the light, Bruce Willis. Walk towards the light.

Speech time

Four score and seven years ago our fathers brought forth on this continent, a new nation, conceived in liberty, and dedicated to the proposition that all men are created equal.
That's how Abraham Lincoln started the Gettysburg address and he got murdered in a theatre.
That's also how I have started my speech but I won't be murdered in a theatre
When I die, it will be an old-time injury, like falling into a threshing machine.

I am always making speeches, but speeches are a waste of time
The only useful speech is one where you enumerate someone's many failures until they burst into tears
But if anyone is bursting into tears today it will be me
I just want to lie naked on a deckchair, fanning myself with divorce papers

I have called this speech 'speech time' so you will know it's time for speeches.
Anything can be a speech if you say it out loud for long enough
This is not freedom of speech, this is just extreme oratorial leeway
It's hot piss, melting the toilet ice

Speeches exist for the purpose of making other people think what you think
But I don't want just *anyone* to be able to think what I think
It's like if paisley were a natural resource, and people had to mine for it
You have to be stupid enough to want to

I've been making a lot of speeches recently because I published a book
And more than a book people like to hear you talk about your book
People don't like books they like speeches
But not this speech ....

{ People don't want to hear poetry, they want to hear people talking about poetry
People don't want to hear poetry, they want to go home and not read poetry and so do I
The only reason for poetry is to have a meadow in which to burn yourself alive in
A picturesque meadow, with bonus violets

I am bored of making speeches
I have to say so many things I don't care about
It reminds me of life
It reminds me of when you are a cowboy and your hat gets too heavy

There is nothing in this world really worth saying
Being clever is a waste of time
I just want to sit around in Swarovski earrings and let old men debate my literary merits
... but I don't even have my ears pierced

A speech is the opposite of a poem
A speech is telling people what to think, but I don't know what should be thought
Sometimes it seems to me like other people aren't even trying to tell the truth
Like, when I watch porn I like it to be the retro kind when you can't see the dick go in

Forget this speech, I'm changing the title
The new title of this speech is 'poem time' because this is poem time not speech time
It's like when it's your first day as a soldier and you show up to the wrong war
Or like sexily cleaning the coliseum with a black feather duster

It's like panicking because your castle is too beautiful
Or an advent calendar for atheists full of empty windows
It's like pouring cold champagne all over your thighs
Or an evil piano that can only be played at midnight

A poem should never be a tourniquet
You have to let the blood goes where it wants
It's like trying to log into your email account but your password makes you too sad
It's like Shakespeare .... etc

I love writing poetry because it gives me casket pleasure
I can feel my death somewhere far off
It's like doing a shot of semen after sex and calling it a chaser
Or when you're a ghost and can feel the wind blow in through your sheetholes

Poetry is like a tuxedo that zips off at the knee
It's my pet boredom ......
I sit in my room with the rain coming down
And I start to *wonder* about my life

Poetry is like pushing a pram through the dawn
But the pram is on fire, because the fire is your baby
It's like having an orgasm every time you hear middle C on a piano
Mozart is just elaborate foreplay to you

It's like upgrading your horse drawn carriage to a better, more technologically advanced horse drawn carriage
Or squeezing your mop into a tropical fish tank
It's like being the Monet of blow jobs .... and losing your boyfriend to the Toulouse-Lautrec of blowjobs
Or a bedside drawer packed with snow

Poetry is a luxury behaviour
Like crying because you're too clever and nobody understands you
It's like cutting your hand at a party and referring to your blood as 'party blood'
It's like: welcome to good behaviour town, population 0

I will already remember you for the rest of my life

Standing on your balcony in winter I think:
I will already remember you for the rest of my life
It's too late now, I know who you are
and what you look like
and must henceforth venture through life recalling you many times
as you continue to make things difficult by reminding yourself to me more and more
by taking me to various locations and describing to me your .... aspirations
some ancient moon smouldering above us
I will always think of you and how it was between us
and the things you did and said

I will think about your ... personality and your ... interests
and the specific colour of your hair and eyes
even if we have a terrific breakup and stop calling each other
I'll still remember you
I won't be able to help it! You're there in my memory
like the concept of opera. Or the Simpsons theme song
like a field of blossoms in an air freshener commercial
sarcastic with light
I will think of your temperament and your enthusiasms
and how you ... looked at me
I will think of all the things you told me about your life

Everything is about to go wrong forever

I know, I can feel it
not just on the wind, but in my blood too
a hundred miniature warning horses galloping through my veins
with evil pink gemstones for eyes
everything is about to get really dark and fucked up
like a series of daytime infomercials directed by Michael Haneke
it already has, I just don't know how yet
and all I can do is sit in my room & wait
for the news, whatever it is, to reach me
and immediately ruin my life
cancer, war, heartbreak
death and venereal disease
I don't know what this impending reckoning is
only that it will haunt me from this point onwards
and become the kind of thing people associate with me for the rest of my life
it will be so bad people will forget I ever wrote poetry
I will be so bad I should probably just give up and legally change my name to
Westpac Family Day Tractor Victim #4

when it happens, I hope it happens quickly
the sooner I know my life is over the better
then I can leave all my things by the side of the road in the night
and retreat into my punishment
because it is a punishment, I can feel that too
for what I don't know
for what I can hardly dare think about
but whatever it was I did, it must have been bad
like burning down an orphanage in my sleep
I am always waiting for the moment in my life
where something so profoundly depressing and pointless will occur
it will prove to me there is no god
and nothing good is able to be recovered
maybe I will have both hands cut off by a helicopter blade and they will fly off
and slap my mother in the face …… twice

maybe I will go back in time but instead of leading the French to victory I will just be forced to toil in the fields for years until I die of some historically accurate disease
maybe my boyfriend will slowly die of cancer
maybe my boyfriend will slowly die of cancer, and just before he dies he will leave me for his beautiful French oncologist who has better hair than me
you may think I'm being melodramatic
but every day the worst thing that ever happened to somebody
is happening to somebody
I feel mine getting closer, and closer
I feel it in the back of my mouth, where all my teeth are slowly turning black

I look around and the world is full of bad omens
75% off knives at the knife emporium
a standard poodle with a wet pink glove in its mouth
I can feel leaves drifting down over my future gravestone
I can feel each one strike, like a hammer on the moon
I hope whatever it is, when it happens
I don't learn anything from it
I hope when I die they say at my funeral
she had a really terrible attitude about the whole thing
and gave up immediately, without even trying
and pushed everyone who loved her away
through a combination of vindictive silence and unprovoked personal attacks
I hope nobody comes to my funeral
except for the undertaker, and my mother
I hope the ham sandwiches which are provided in my deluxe bereavement care package
go uneaten & have to be redirected
to a landfill somewhere, to turn white in the heat
I hope when I die, God
with a wild, bad look in his eye
will rinse my blood off the bonnet of his sports utility vehicle
and drive off into the sunset
whistling the theme song to Midnight Cowboy

I want to get high my whole life with you

i feel it in my leather hotpant pockets
i feel it in my anime wind blowing through an alpine tennis resort
overcome with wildflowers
i feel it in my ironic valley girl hairflip
i feel it in my admittedly limited knowledge of the Roman mythologies
i feel it in my biopic about a corrupt alcoholic educational resource salesman
advertising increasingly less and less educational resources
i want to get high my whole life with you
i feel it in my anime wind blowing through an alpine tennis resort
overcome with wildflowers AGAIN, and the poem isn't even halfway over yet
so what if my blood is the wind
so what if I love you so much I am becoming stupid
my heart melting like red candles on Satan's birthday cake

i want to get high with you out the back of our family funerals
i want to get high with you at an industrial carpet outlet store
i want to get high with you at the top of the Grand Canyon and pretend like
you are going to push me in and scream and pretend to try not to get pushed in
even though I know you pushing me in is the last thing you want because if you
did that I'd die and you don't want me to die
I love you so much I tell you about it
I love you so much I have already picked out my grave and written your name
on it when you laugh in the dark
it fills up the corners of the room with a thousand upside-down cartoon bats

how dare you be the kind of person I would immediately fall completely in love
    with and be devastated if you left
how dare you come and do that
your eyes
like two black cats
licking their assholes
in the hot morning sun of my face

O this feeling has drenched my bones
and turned my skeleton pink
with you I feel my mind changing
with you I feel my blood changing
I want to get really good at woodwork
I want to get really good at woodwork
and go into the forest
and cut up some logs
and make you a beautiful house to live in

Waste my life

sleep, boredom, gossip, cruelty
imaginary feuds and small resentments
various, complex plans that amount to nothing
at some point, every poet has to admit art is just a distraction from the boredom of life

every morning I get dressed
and I walk past the road outside the Salvation Army
overflowing with toys and clothes and plastic crap
I think they probably deserve it for being so explicitly homophobic in their core organizational values

I work all day in a bookshop
each night when I come home
it's dark, and the rain is falling
covering the world in black diamonds
some days I feel so deep inside my life I don't think I'll ever get out again

I never read the Russians but I have read most of the Babysitters Club
I can't remember the meaning of poetry
other than it's a broken telephone
with which to call the dead
and tell them a joke

life is great
it's like being given a rare and historically significant flute
and using it to beat a harmless old man to death with

I used to think the more something hurt, the more meaningful it was
but I never learned anything useful from pain
I just drank a bottle of wine and tried to fall asleep
when you're unhappy you can't think
pain is just boredom with the stars turned up

there's not much I like in this world
I'm always walking away too early in a conversation and having to
yell apologetically back over my shoulder

I don't think good art comes from happiness either
but who said good art was the point

Jealousy

anytime someone I am dating ever mentions someone they used to love
in a semi-nostalgic or non-cynical way
I immediately want to drive my car head-first into a swamp full of battery acid
ruining Christmas for everyone!!!
it's so unreasonable
to be afraid of so many sad and distant women
who have escaped into the future
only occasionally looking back through naturally thick eyelashes
when I think about the possibility
the person I'm currently with has ever been remotely romantically interested
in another person ever
I felt a great self-antagonism
for being the kind of woman who came afterwards
like a bad sequel with a higher budget
O I feel sorry for the people I love and where it is I am taking them
because I don't think I'm good enough
I think it's okay to admit the people you love are better than you
I wouldn't date anyone who wasn't
imagine dating someone worse than yourself on purpose
that's the kind of fucked up thing only everyone I've ever loved would do

I am so in love with you I want to lie down in the middle of a major public intersection and cry

is not how you are supposed to start love poems
but I'm too far gone
to work up to it gently

your naked back in the mirror
has cured at least 3-4 major diseases

for you, I would set myself on fire in a smoke detector factory
for you, I would ride through the mall on a Segway knocking juices out of the hands of thirsty real estate agents

your lungs like Christmas stockings waiting for Santa to climb down the chimney & put cancer in
your face like the face of a dead French revolutionary in an outdated children's textbook
my stupid heart .... like a snowglobe .... filled with blood

If you left me, I would be forced to gaze despairingly into the middle distance
If you left me I would be forced to emotionally distance myself from the situation as a self-preservation technique until eventually I healed enough to be able to consider romantic relationships with other people, all the time secretly resenting you for failing to sustain your attraction to me despite the totally involuntary & uncontrollable nature of human desire

your teeth like a graveyard .... in springtime
your tongue like a mattress .... in a graveyard .... in springtime
your tongue on my cunt like a mattress .... in a graveyard .... in springtime
my pubic hair like the black carpet on the titanic
my ass .... like an ass buffet

you put me in a friendly but uncompromising headlock
you bite me all over my neck and shoulders

i don't know how to write a love poem
because love is indescribable
it's this feeling you get
when your mind gets hot
and everything else gets insignificant .... with diamonds on it
and you have to laugh and laugh at things in your second-hand dress

the slow rising of your eyelid
like a girl's skirt

my eyes like two envelopes stuffed with snow and no return address
my eyes like pair of pale blue cowboy boots walking slowly down a city street towards you

it's like
you've finally found someone that interests you
and you get more and more interested
like a fascinating disease
it's like
for some reason, you have to think of the wild west all the time
but it doesn't make any sense???
because you don't really care about the wild west!!!!

it's better than tv
to look at someone and feel so much happiness
your smile a single arrow, quivering in a tree trunk

it's like .... life is not a punishment
and sometimes good things happen for no reason
I stare and stare at you like you were a distant mountain in a homeopathic video game
with rare and medicinal flowers on it

I knew I loved you when you showed me your Minecraft world

It wasn't the upside-down crosses in your mansion
or even the lone, giant cigarette burning in the sky
you walked me around and I watched the back of your head
suddenly overcome by the feeling of knowing
I was beyond what could be recovered from
the dark pixels of the forest vibrating in a virtual wind
distant panpipe music blowing through your speakers
It's not that I didn't love you before
it is just – there are some things which cannot be said
and some feelings which, if articulated too early
and forced towards the surface go blind
& it's better to hold them off, or wait them out
& never say their name aloud until the pressure of what is unspoken
becomes impossible to hold back
and articulates itself within the body
like mice, running wild through a field of burning grass.
The train disappears underground and comes back up again
The cigarette distributes its vague cancers into the sky
Outside the sky is firing navy shadows like a T-shirt gun
And spring is on the wind like wifi
When I was miserable you came and showed me card tricks
When the moon was full we pissed into the bushes like animals
I watch you sleep, like a security guard looking at a famous painting
with a searchlight
walk me to the graveyard on the edge of your map
nothing must hurt you, not even me

Watching six seasons of the Nanny while my long-term relationship slowly fell apart

Watching six seasons of the Nanny while my long-term relationship fell apart
Was more self-inflicted boredom than nostalgia
As Maxwell chased Fran up and down the staircase with a frying pan
And I lay in bed, listening to the distant sound of trains
Pulling their shit-for-brains cargo through the dark

There are some months when all art feels worthless
And life feels thin, and weak and full of spite
And the pastel hysteria of spring of outside the window
Just makes me wince with disappointment and rage
And the total, mind-numbing futility of it all
Often, I think about the man who walked into the National Gallery
And punched a hole straight into a ten million-dollar Monet painting
Of a sailboat, drifting down a river of autumn leaves
And got sent to prison for five years

There's nothing in this world more boring than heartbreak
It's like a tax audit of the soul
And what once seemed rare and poignant
And full of emotional promise
Just makes me want to dose myself to the brim with horse tranquilizers
And take a long vacation to skeleton town

There's only so much sitting by the window
Begging the moon for punishment
You can take, before you have to get mad
And stride up and down the toiletries aisles of the grocery store
Wishing every old woman painstakingly reading the back of a Listerine packet
An expedient journey to hell
and all the poets you loved
reveal themselves to be little bitches

Whose constant need to reupholster their pain
seems sad & extravagant
like grief factories, polluting the local waterways with pathos and nuance

The present has overflowed and turned the whole past bad
Ancient Greece, art nouveau, the entire Italian renaissance
All ruined
Monet too, with his surfeit of waterlilies
Wilting in the heat like a loose-leaf salad

I sit like Nostradamus
In my kingdom of disappointment
Burning down the cities of the future
Going through my google calendar
listing all the bad things to come

I have come back from the dead to tell you that I love you

I have come to move your cups transparently through the air
To tremble in the corner of your eye like a fuzzy diamond

I am shaking off my worms like cowboy tassels!!!
I have put your bedsheet over my head and cut both eyeholes out

Lilacs, snakes, disco-balls, birdbaths
Alligators, tennis courts, self-respect, nothing

Green tin roofs shining all along the river
& the palliative stars above

I lie underground, sprouting flowers like a rural Liberace
my tumours like pink bells ringing into oblivion,

I have come back one last time to look at you
Your beauty is heavy on my eyes, like tiny anvils

I have come back to our house on the last day of summer
I have come back to say I love you, and I'm sorry for being dead

Untitled 404

(After a Cindy Sherman Photograph)

Recently someone scolded me for speaking about Cindy Sherman because
    Cindy Sherman was an instrument of the patriarchy
Like an evil saxophone, that only plays hold music for a bank
Bad financial jazz pouring out of the telephone
O sometimes I get so tired I want to blow the stars out, one by one

Every year people demand to know what art is feminist and what art is
    un-feminist
Sometimes I wonder if it's ethical to be a woman at all
It's a great stupidity to waste your life on right-seeming behaviour
Like putting a coin in a jukebox that only plays whale song

I like this picture because it reminds me of loneliness
And the great, unspecific boredom of life
It's the expression I get every time someone tries to hold me accountable
    for my artistic wrongdoings
The critical theorists advancing, with black leather pompoms

Once there was a time in which I had many ideologies
Many self-pleasing ideologies with which to chastise others
The theme of these ideologies was: however wrong you are, that is the exact
    amount I am right by
I felt them in my blood like too much money

Once upon a time, I had many ideologies
Many superior ideologies, with which to cheerfully educate
    my family and friends
Forget crying myself to sleep, I wanted to cry everyone else there
Then drive off in my Cadillac, my black wig blowing

Once upon a time I had many ideologies
And by ideologies I mean specific ideas about things other people should and
    shouldn't do
But proving yourself right is a bad career
Then you have to prove yourself even righter, in a blue satin pantsuit

Sometimes the world is so backwards all you can do is stare
Stare and stare, from out behind your waterproof mascara
Oh it's a great responsibility to be your own misogynist
There are so many beaded handbags with which to oppress yourself

{ I don't think the great project of art is ideological messaging time
  Like Monet, spelling 'fuck you' in waterlilies
  All I want is to pour my eyes into the world
  The sunset blazing overhead like too much eyeshadow

People are always on the lookout for new ideologies with which to punish
    themselves
Contemporary ideologies, studded with hashtags
It's like not being able to wear a sexy nurse outfit unless you apply for a sexy
    medical licence
You have to take someone's blood pressure with your skirt hiked up

There are a lot of punishments in this world
And some of these punishments look a lot like day to day life
Some things cannot be transformed, only endured
The moon shining over all of us, with its clean white handrail

The imperative to be correct is the great failure of the left
Sometimes you just want to wash iceberg lettuce in quiet despair
It's like buying a second wig, and putting it on over the wig
    you're already wearing
You cry and cry, impressing no-one

Pyramid scheme

the other day I was thinking about the term Pyramid Scheme, and why they
called it Pyramid Scheme and not triangle scheme,
I asked you what you thought
you thought it added a certain gravitas, and linked the idea of economic
        prosperity
with some of history's greatest archaeological achievements
unconsciously suggesting a silent wealth of gold and heat
a triangle is two dimensional, and therefore
a less striking mental image than the idea of a third dimension of financial fraud
which is how many dimensions of financial fraud the term pyramid scheme
        suggests
but I had to pause for a second at the financial fraud part
because it occurred to me I didn't know what pyramid schemes really were
I knew they had something to do with people getting money from nothing
like
the person at the top of the pyramid scheme, or more accurately
triangle scheme, acquires a number of investors and takes their money
and then pays the first lot of investors with the money from another bunch of
investors
and so on and so forth
all the way to the bottom of the triangle
or pyramid face
which is the kind of stupid thing that happens
if you keep your money in a pyramid and not a bank account
although if you ask me banks are the real pyramid schemes after all
or was love the real pyramid scheme? I can't remember

maybe its better to keep your money in a pyramid than a bank
and I should shop around and compare the interest rates on different pyramids
maybe I should open up a savings pyramid
with a whole bunch of trapdoors and malarias
to keep the financial anthropologists

I mean bankers out
my emeralds cooling under the ground like beautiful women's eyes

I think this was supposed to be a metaphor for something
but I can't remember where I was going with it
and now it's been swept away by the winds of
whatever
but knowing me, it was probably love
That great dark blue sex hope that keeps coming true
That cartoon black castle with a single bird flying over it

I don't know where this poem ends
how far below the sand
but it's still early evening
and you and I are a little drunk
you answer the phone
you pour me a drink
i know you hate the domestic in poetry but you should have thought of that
    before you invited me to move in with you
i used to think arguments were the same as honesty
i used to think screaming was the same as passion
i used to think pain was meaningful
i no longer think pain is meaningful
i never learned anything good from being unhappy
i never learned anything good from being happy either
the way i feel about you has nothing to do with learning
it has nothing to do with anything
but i feel it down in the corners of my sarcophagus
i feel it in my sleep
even when i am not thinking about you
you are still pouring through my blood, like fire through an abandoned
    hospital ward
these coins are getting heavy on my eyes
it has been a great honour and privilege to love you
it is a great honour and privilege to eat cold pizza on your steps at dawn

love is so stupid: it's like punching the sun
and having a million gold coins rain down on you
which you don't even have to pay tax on
because sun money is free money
and I'm pretty sure there are no laws about that
but I would pay tax
because I believe hospitals and education
and the arts should be publicly funded
even this poem
when I look at you, my eyes are two identical neighbourhood houses on fire
when I look at you my eyes bulge out of my skull like a dog in a cartoon
when I am with you
an enormous silence descends upon me
and i feel like i am sinking into the deepest part of my life
we walk down the street, with the grass blowing back and forth
i have never been so happy

Acknowledgements

Thanks to the Sarah Broom Foundation for awarding me the Sarah Broom Prize for a selection of poems, which form the basis of this chapbook, and Carol Ann Duffy for selecting my work. Thanks to everyone at Victoria University Press and Penguin UK for all their support. Thanks to Unity Books, particularly Tilly Lloyd for her eccentric & generous patronage. Thanks to The Arts Foundation and Creative New Zealand for their financial help, allowing me the time to work on these poems. Thanks to the first publishers of these pieces, *The Spinoff, Queen Mobs, Pouch Magazine*, The Wellington City Gallery & Cindy Sherman, *Fuse Box and Lichtungen*. Thanks to my partner, Rhydian Thomas.